INTO THE WORLD OF LOVE

FASHITH ABDUL

Copyright © Fashith Abdul
All Rights Reserved.

This book has been published with all efforts taken to make the material error-free after the consent of the author. However, the author and the publisher do not assume and hereby disclaim any liability to any party for any loss, damage, or disruption caused by errors or omissions, whether such errors or omissions result from negligence, accident, or any other cause.

While every effort has been made to avoid any mistake or omission, this publication is being sold on the condition and understanding that neither the author nor the publishers or printers would be liable in any manner to any person by reason of any mistake or omission in this publication or for any action taken or omitted to be taken or advice rendered or accepted on the basis of this work. For any defect in printing or binding the publishers will be liable only to replace the defective copy by another copy of this work then available.

"Where love is great, the littlest doubts are fear;

where little fears grows great, great love grows there."

William Shakespeare, Hamlet.

Contents

Contents

Fantasy

1. In A Dream World

Our nights shined like a rainbow
And our path directed us to dreamland.

We slipped into each others soul
And saw shades of heaven.

In the sea of love
We swam like dolphins.

Every second together
Ensured a lifetime of eternal happiness.

2. Love Invited Us

In a sacred world
Where only love exists
We were invited as guests.
Like the rain showers
Angels greeted us with love showers.

As guests, we were too hesitant and shy
But their love rinsed away all our insecurities.

Every episode of each day
Taught us the unknown secrets of love
And helped us to love even more.

3. As Super Couple

On a bright night
Under the moonlight
We made love until the sun flashed.

We kissed in a loop
And hugged without a pause.

As super couple
We moved in & around in the fairy-tale world
And were crowned as the king & queen
Of the fantasy world.

Our love life witnessed multi innings
With many years of togetherness
And our love dictionary got updated with exclusive new
meanings.

Wish

4. A Soulful Wish

Like the rain in a hot summer
Be my long wished happiness.

I promise to be your sunset
As long as the sun rises.

An end too far
Or a route without an end
Let's pen our chapters together.

A movie night
Or a heated argument
Let us remain "Us" forever.

5. Our Couple Goals

Cold showers on a winter night
And a long drive with short stories.

Several exchanges of snicker bites
And very rare special poems.

Rain dance with slow music
And karaoke nights with broken voices.

A home filled with happiness
And a life filled with kisses and hugs.

6. Be Mine

I want you beside
When this world turns deserted.

Be my hope
When I lose all the strength.

Be as my wings
When I try to fly.

'Be mine' in a parallel universe
And also in a devil's hell.

Long Distance

7. Too Far To Hold

Deep in my thoughts
You bloom like an angel.

Many miles apart
You live like a princess.

Between fairy-tale dreams and harsh reality
My poor heart juggles.

For your tight hugs and divine kisses
My innocent soul longs.

8. Let's Meet Soon My Love

A dozen of mails
And a bunch of gifts
Yet nothing fills our hearts.

From drives to walks
Hugs and kisses
Cuddles and quarrels
Everything awaits us.

So let's meet soon my love!

9. Happily In A Long Distance

Through video calls
We sculpted our love story
And with tons of messages
We built our secret treasure.

Virtual hugs are part
Of our daily rituals
And her innocent blush
Is my daily dose of energy booster.

I miss her presence at times
Yet her absence enhances our love to new extents.

Crush

10. Lost My Heart In A War

Lost my heart in a war
A war between her eyes and my soul.

Like a kid was tied between
Candies and toys.

In love? or a passing cloud?
My mind was in an unstable state.

Yet again lost my heart in a war
A war between her smile and my senses.

11. From A Stranger To My Secret Crush

In a pink salwar
Saw your first glimpse.

No butterflies in the stomach
No ultra fast heartbeats
But for a moment
Everything paused.

Our eyes didn't meet
But I wish our hearts were hugged.

A teenage infatuation
Or maybe a cinematic "Love at first sight"
I don't know how to name it.

But all I know is
I want you now and forever.

12. Few Magical Minutes

We met in a crowded bus depot
Between two buses.

I turned mute
Purposefully to unmute her.

I could hear sounds
From all corners
Yet my mind
Was hooked to her melodious tune.

I can feel the chills
Running on my nerves.

I can feel the crave
Of my heart.

It wasn't planned
Neither it wasn't a date
But it was indeed
'Few magical minutes'.

Proposal

13. And She Said Yes

I don't know
Whether we will travel around the world
But I can promise
To count the stars together every night.

I don't believe in fancy dates
But I can ensure
To love you every single day.

I don't know
Whether I will be available 24/7
But I can promise
To be your everything for 365 days.

So to light our dreams
And to share many showers
Can we turn us?

14. Love Journey

A bunch of movie nights
Few rare candlelight dinners
And an infinite number of pillow fights.

Selfies and couple goals
To long drives and surprises.

All these are chapters
In our destined love journey.

Will, you be "Mine,"
To travel in this journey?

15. Wish To Be Your Soulmate

A short drive
Or a long walk
Will ensure our hands are held tight.

A dreamy night
Or a frightful nightmare
Will caress you with warm hugs.

With a room filled with roses
Or with a fridge filled with candies
Will try to enlighten all your dark days.

To execute my promises
And to fulfill all your wishes
Will you accept me as your soulmate?

Long Drive

16. We Drove A Very Long Mile

In a compact sedan
We drove a very long mile
With fewer words
And with more bliss feels.

Our eyes made love,
And our thoughts remained frozen.
The wheels rolled to the tunes
And our heartbeats collided.

In a compact sedan
We drove a very long mile
With fewer words
And with more bliss feels.

We stopped halfway
To gaze at the aesthetic view
And to inhale fresh natural air.
We shared bites of lays
And swapped KitKat for a munch.

17. A Special Affair

In a highway
Our hearts were flying high
And the wheels were singing a song.

Greenish trees
And deep blue seas
Were icing to the eyes.

Roadside tender coconut
And spicy raw mangoes
Exhaled our thirsty breaths.

A calm wind
And her silky hair
Made love on the air.

With every passing kilometre
The long drive
With my long-lasting soul
Ensured a special affair
To remember forever.

18. She & He

She: A long drive?

He: Why not a full night drive?

She: Will rest on your lap,
And will listen to the lullaby of your heartbeats.

He: Will plant kisses on your cheeks,
And will inhale your sweet scent.

She: Will cuddle at every halt,
And will spoil your hair.

He: Will hold you tight,
Till I fall asleep.

She: Will whisper in your ears,
And will dance together in dreams.

He: Can't wait anymore!
To turn the boring night,
Into a dream night.

Kiss

19. Our First Kiss

Not under a moonlight
With the flashes of stars.

Neither in a bed
Sprinkled with rose petals.

Not in a dark theatre
In the corner couple seat.

But our lips met
For the first time
In a fully covered
Tinted closed car.

20. An Instant Booster

A dry morning
And a drained body
Craved for an instant energy booster.

Like a thirsty penguin
My heart scouted for an ocean.

While I was drowning without any rescue
You flashed like a granted wish
Straight out of the heavens.

With your creamy touch
And soul-soothing kiss
You powered my drained soul instantly.

21. One Divine Kiss In A Holy Night

A calm night
Accompanied with rain showers.

Freezing eyes
And nervous faces.

The tune of our heartbeats
Sounds crystal clear.

I slightly pull you closer
To make our lips meet.

We kissed like there's no tomorrow
And our lips were glued like two magnets.

If it was a dream
We would have remained unmoved
But this wasn't a dream
Hence we had no choice but to end.

Fights

22. Our Silly Fights

We fought for candies
And for pillows.

We fought in texts
And with fists.

Few for silly reasons
And some for no reason.

We loved to irritate
And found love in hate.

23. On A Heated Night

In a roller coaster
We peeked through a secret window.

The gates of hell awaited for us
And the bricks of heaven were falling apart.

Like a popcorn
Our anger cells popped up.
To stay in love we dreamed
Instead, we were glued in hate.

24. Never Parted Ways

From Netflix series
Kitkat sharings
And bedtime kisses.

To crush stories
Fan fights
And Instagram reels.

Our life discovered multi-shades.

We cared
We loved
And we also shared a little hatred.

Few bright nights
And many dark days.

We stood strong at all times.

We had conflicts
Ego peeked in at times
But nothing rifted us.

As life partners
As soulmates
We remained 'Us'
And never parted ways.

Breakup

25. One Great Chapter

In my darkest world
You appeared as an angel of light.

The stare of your eyes
Brought spark in my smile.

The tune of your voice
Healed my broken heart.

All I ever wished since then
Was to be with you and only you.

Days and months
We loved and overloved.

I wish it to be a nightmare
But no all this finally came to an end
As one great chapter.

26. Our Happy Memories

Endless night talks
Secret night meets
And husky love songs
A collection of blissful memories.

Wish we traversed more
In a dream world
Making fairy-tale dreams come true.

Wish we didn't break our hearts
Wish we didn't weep the whole night.

We hoped to be the story
Of 'Our happy world'
But ended as chapters
Of 'Our happy memories'.

27. Detached

You were my dream
When I had only nightmares.

You were my soul
When my energies got drained.

You were my path
When my heart wandered without a direction.

But now you're a memory
When I long to be yours forever.

Sorry

28. A day to remember

Today is our fifth anniversary!
I muttered in a frightful tone.

You have ruined it!
She retorted back in a firm tone.

Yes, I did.
Indeed it feels so frustrating
But I wish,
To take a nap
On your lap.

Maybe a slap
On your face
That is what I wish to grant.

Her eyes popped out in anger.

Without delaying any further
I hugged her tightly
And smooched
Until we lost our breaths.

With happy teary eyes
And soulful exchanges of sorries
We fed each other
A plateful of sweetly baked
Chocolate brownies.

29. A Sudden Strange Storm

A sudden strange storm
Gifted new sets of alarms.

Her eyes ignited a fire
Yet she stayed calm as ice.

I whispered sorry into her reddish cute ears
And planted a cheeky forehead kiss.

Neither worked
In turn, our hearts were caged.

30. Sorry & Thank You

Sorry for not gifting roses
And for spoiling your outfits.

Sorry for not sharing gulab jamuns
And for serving cold pizzas.

Sorry for not whispering
My secret wishes
And for taking long rides
In damaged motorbikes.

Sorry for not overloving
And for always misunderstanding.

Sorry for being your mismatch
And thank you for being my dream match.

www.ingramcontent.com/pod-product-compliance
Lightning Source LLC
Chambersburg PA
CBHW061402160726
47995CB00001B/429